THE LITTLE BOOK OF
HSP WISDOM

THE
LITTLE BOOK
OF HSP
WISDOM

A quick reference guide to life for highly
sensitive people

BARBARA ALLEN-WILLIAMS

The manufacturer's authorised representative in the EU for product safety is Authorised Rep
Compliance Ltd, 71 Lower Baggot Street, Dublin D02 P593 Ireland
(www.arccompliance.com)

Troubador Publishing Ltd
Unit E2 Airfield Business Park
Harrison Road, Market Harborough
Leicestershire LE16 7UL
Tel: 0116 279 2299
Email: books@troubador.co.uk
Web: www.troubador.co.uk

ISBN 978-1-83628-318-8

British Library Cataloguing in Publication Data.
A catalogue record for this book is available from the British Library.

Typeset in 11pt Garamond Pro by Troubador Publishing Ltd, Leicester, UK

Our deepest fear is not that we are inadequate.
Our deepest fear is that we are powerful beyond
measure. It is our light, not our darkness, that most
frightens us. We ask ourselves 'who am I to be
brilliant, gorgeous, talented, fabulous?' Actually,
who are you not to be?

— *MARIANNE WILLIAMSON*

CONTENTS

INTRODUCTION

*O*ver recent years, high sensitivity, or *sensory processing sensitivity*, has become fairly well known as a concept. There are many websites, books, articles and videos out there now that go into this topic in varying (and sometimes questionable) levels of accuracy, detail and helpfulness. Some of them are laced with attention-grabbing and provocative headlines, but many leave one with more questions than answers. I think the reason for that is that they might not quite have the melding of immediacy, facts and the bigger picture that highly sensitive people (HSPs) really need (and that Elaine Aron, PhD, created so well with her first book).

In order to navigate a way forward in a world where there are a lot of opinions but few down-to-earth, common-sense hints about how to live a real and content life as a mature HSP, I felt there was a need for a simple book of common HSP wisdom, one that is easy to access. Of course, the fact is that life is not always happy, but even so, that doesn't stop us from developing maturity and know-how about living an authentic, satisfying HSP life whilst taking each day at a time with its joys and challenges. Part of being happy is knowing that you will find a way to manage the next challenge, even if you are not happy about that challenge. It can be surprising to many HSPs to find out that your sensitivity actually sets you up to be more likely to find solutions and a way to be happy, giving you a reason to have confidence in your ability to navigate a way forward.

This book is for anyone who has found out they might be highly sensitive, but who wants a quick reference resource for navigating life's tasks and growth ahead as they meander towards a more authentic sensitive life. I have deliberately chosen to keep each chapter fairly short, offering some straightforward 'dos' and 'don'ts' with explanations and guidance about doing life as an HSP. It's a kind of 'do this' and 'don't do that' book – a 'no-nonsense HSP book' – with easy chapter headings, a quick discussion and some tips here and there. Because of its simplicity, this book might come across in a very direct style, so be prepared for some straight talking at times. It is not just about 'how to survive' or 'overcoming problems', it is a book to prepare you for the journey to HSP maturity.

There are quotes in this book from writers on the topic of high sensitivity and the bigger picture. There are also quotes from me (placed underneath the pictures). The anonymous quotes are from HSPs who have written to me for the purpose of this book, with feedback about their path towards wholeness or maturity as a highly sensitive person. They have asked not to be identified, but their contribution is very much appreciated.

Of course, the ideas in this book are merely suggestions, based on my own experience, journey and learning over the last thirty years. If they don't fit with what you want, then do things differently; how you do your life is your own choice. The resource section lists some books, websites and other resources that might assist you in addressing the topics covered in this book, including titles of some of the research papers that point to factual elements of this temperament trait. However, this book is a little book of HSP wisdom about living your life, so no attempt is being made here to regurgitate the scientific data that is out there if you wish to look it up. You can look up more information on Elaine Aron, PhD's website, www.hsperson.com, if this will be helpful to you.

You can use the contents page to look up the things that are pertinent to you at this time (ah yes, those things one tries to find out about in urgency because in the busyness of life in the dominant culture, we convinced ourselves we didn't need to read about it ahead of time!). There is no particular order required to make the most of this book, just choose what interests you and go from there.

ACKNOWLEDGEMENTS

I would like to thank Elaine N Aron, PhD, for doing the work of research and writing that has helped so many highly sensitive people to have a better understanding of their trait and a reason to be proud of their difference. The reframing of the experiences of over a billion people is a massive achievement and serves as inspiration to many, like me, who wish to help underpin and support the sea change that the world needs right now. Thank you, Elaine, from the bottom of my heart.

My deep gratitude goes to Jacquelyn Strickland, friend and colleague of many years, whose work continues to inspire HSPs around the world through the HSP Gathering Retreats she and Elaine Aron co-created; and who has modelled courage, wisdom and compassion in a world that offers so many challenges to our highly sensitive nature.

I would also like to offer my profound thanks to Karen, my friend of thirty years, who encouraged me to write, offered her belief and didn't let me give up. Thanks also to Theresa, Rosie, Georgina and Janet who have offered a listening ear when I have needed to vent my aspirations and frustrations.

Thank you to the HSPs who wrote to me to answer some questions about what learning about their trait has meant to them and who are quoted anonymously in parts of this book.

Appreciation to Bill Allen, who encouraged me to make a proper start as an author and thanks also to my colleague Ildiko Davies for her dedicated support and encouragement for my work with HSPs over the years.

My profound thanks also go to my therapist, Alison, who supported me with compassion and without judgement for many years and who walked alongside me on my emotional journey towards authentic sensitive living. And, of course, deep appreciation to my husband Mike, who put up with me being away writing when I needed to be alone with my thoughts.

Without all these people, it would have been much harder to have found my voice.

1

SOME BASIC BUT IMPORTANT FACTS ABOUT HIGH SENSITIVITY

(It's a real thing and so much of it is positive)

This temperament trait is normal and has genetically influenced features that differentiate approximately 20% of the human population. Elaine Aron, PhD, published a paper on this topic as long ago as 1997 and that paper was a springboard for much future research (see chapter on resources and Elaine Aron's website www.hsperson.com for links to papers on the facts that follow). I am going to summarise below the main characteristics of high sensitivity for the sake of simplicity.

The trait of high sensitivity is also called *sensory processing sensitivity* and includes unusually strong qualities under the following headings:

- Depth of processing

- Over-arousal
- Emotional depth and deep empathy
- Sensitivity to subtleties

High sensitivity is found in over one hundred other species, in a similar ratio of 15–20%. The trait is characterised by a more finely tuned nervous system, including 'pause to check' behaviour (an evolutionary survival strategy), strong ability for social and emotional awareness of self and others, high situational adaptability, creativity, noticing of details, plus deep and complex processing of thoughts and emotions, making links that are not obvious to others.

High sensitivity is spread evenly amongst males and females. 70% of HSPs are introverts. A recent study showed that about half of HSPs have the high sensation-seeking trait (a trait characterised by novelty-seeking or adventure-seeking). You can find out more about the high sensation-seeking trait in the book *Thrill* by Tracy Cooper, PhD. Introversion, extroversion and high sensation seeking are not 'diagnoses', they are normal traits found in healthy people and in HSPs as well as non-HSPs. Highly sensitive people can be found in all of the Myers-Briggs personality types, although there are more in certain types than others (INFP, INFJ and more). Myers-Briggs created a way to type personality differences; you can find out more about these types through a quick internet search, but the site 16 Personalities is quite useful for very basic self-typing. Jacquelyn Strickland also offers sessions exploring the Myers-Briggs types with an HSP overlay that you might find enlightening. HSPs often come across as intelligent and deep thinkers. They are not always more intelligent than others; however, they tend to do more with what they have due to their depth of processing and tolerance of complexity; in this way, their intelligence often shows up as a kind of wisdom and creativity, born of deep reflection, empathy and analysis.

HSPs have *vantage sensitivity*. That means they are capable of gaining more from good environments and experiences than the other 80%. They also have *differential susceptibility*, so they can also be more affected by negative environments and experiences than the other 80%.

HSPs have a tendency to be more affected by caffeine, alcohol, some medications, recreational drugs and unhealthy environmental influences. They do not tend to have more illnesses than others; however, they are stressed more easily when living a life or lifestyle that is not suited to them, which can, in turn, affect their general well-being or the progress of any illnesses they already have. HSPs also need more downtime and sleep and are more affected by parenting quality than others. With good parenting, HSPs tend to be less shy, more calm and more adaptable than the other 80%, but don't do as well as the other 80% if they have been raised in harsh or abusive environments.

Overall, HSPs tend to be conscientious, have high-level executive brain functioning (leading to good decision-making), show very good intuitive social and relationship skills and empathy, have creative strength and, as children, can have wisdom beyond their years (see Linda Silverman's paper on *The Moral Sensitivity of Gifted Children and the Evolution of Society*).

> You are more aware than others of subtleties. This
> is mainly because your brain processes information
> and reflects on it more deeply.
> — ELAINE N ARON, PHD

The facts above have been discovered through diligent scientific study, but in everyday life, what are HSPs like as people and how would we know if we met a highly sensitive person, you might ask?

Recognising an HSP is not entirely straightforward since they tend to vary as much as any other group in personality, but their temperament trait influences them as a group in various recognisable ways. There are a number of things that make HSPs visible – personally, one of the most common things I look for is the way they manage to make others feel comfortable – that takes skill, observation, empathy and responsiveness. Below is a list of things that you might notice about a highly sensitive person. Of course, HSPs are unlikely to have all of the qualities in the list below in one person, they are individuals and their life history, culture or unhealed wounds might make these qualities harder to spot.

- They respond more deeply to situations and their own and others' emotions than most (even if they may have learnt not to show it for cultural reasons) and have a high level of *cognitive empathy*.
- They tend to be deeply compassionate, thoughtful and wise. This makes them popular as friends or confidants.

- They are adept in awareness of social cues and interpreting language, emotional inflection, facial cues and body language. To others, they sometimes even seem to be able to read people's minds (this is due to their intuitive and observational skills, not 'special powers').
- They notice all sorts of subtleties that others often miss.
- They can be very creative and see links between things that others might not, having a unique perspective.
- They like to think things through before acting or speaking and will take their time. This usually results in making better decisions than most.
- They tend to give very good-quality attention, taking a deep interest in people and showing that they are listening.
- They enjoy humour, but not cruel humour.
- They consider deep issues, world problems and innovative ideas constantly, although observers often do not know they are doing this. Some of this processing might keep them awake at night and often continues when they are asleep.
- They can understand many people's points of view and, despite their enjoyment of learning, are intelligently aware that they do not know everything.
- They catch on to ideas quickly.
- They can get bored easily, especially in conversations that lack depth or meaning for them. It is common for HSPs to deal with boredom by daydreaming or disappearing off on their own for a walk.

- They rarely seek the limelight, even when it is deserved, although they appreciate recognition for their contributions.
- They often have a sense of the spiritual about them, even if they are not religious.
- Their creativity and gifts might extend into the sciences, the arts, writing or acting, yet the public attention this brings might be more stressful for them than most.
- They will often feel drawn to careers that involve supporting or educating others, or a job that deals with subtle or fine details, public safety or service.
- HSPs' focus is usually very good, except in environments that are particularly distracting, so they often seek out quiet spaces to work or study.
- They can see what is going on in the moment whilst also being aware of the bigger picture.
- They are comfortable with looking at the long-term outcomes of decisions that they make now.
- They will value time in nature, opportunities to appreciate beauty in the arts, music, and time alone for rest and processing. Their natural intensity means they may choose to withdraw for periods of time to recharge their social batteries, even if they are extroverts and even if they have been doing something enjoyable.
- They value harmony, gentleness, honesty and fairness and can feel distressed when these are absent in personal or societal interactions.
- They tend to be very clear on their values.

- They are more affected by the good things, as well as negative things.
- They are grittily realistic, even though their values might seem somewhat naïve to others.
- They tend to hold high standards for themselves and have high hopes and expectations of others.
- Trustworthiness is high on their relational agenda. Their love attachments tend to be deep, sometimes spiritual, and they invest a lot in them. For this reason, grief and loss can be particularly difficult for them.
- They have more intense responses to alcohol, caffeine and some drugs and are more quickly overwhelmed or overstimulated when exposed to hectic or harsh environments.
- They can be very protective of their sleep.
- They prefer gaps between tasks and activities, to rest their nervous system and reset.
- They can make good leaders and tend towards service rather than dominance or flamboyance.

2

GENERAL MATURITY AND EMPOWERMENT: STANDING UP TO YOUR FULL HEIGHT AS AN HSP

In order to be able to find our place in the world as sensitive people, one of the things we most need is to be who we really are. When we are authentic, we can stand up to our full height and use our strengths, both on our own behalf and that of others. HSPs have some things in common as a group but, as individuals, we tend to vary as much as the rest of the human population, so knowing ourselves well will make a big difference to success in finding our way. Finding a way to maturity and having a sense of empowerment to be who we are, will lead to being the best version of ourselves. Whilst this might apply to all human beings, it is particularly important for HSPs, since we are a minority that can be hugely affected by the dominant (non-HSP) culture. We have natural needs that, when met, will underpin our development and the role we play in our family and community.

The work of moving towards maturity and empowerment is not easy, neither should it be. Important things are not easy and take practice. But the good news is that HSPs have an enhanced capacity to learn, not only from experience, but from watching others' experiences. We notice the subtleties, we learn lessons quickly, we are deeply reflective. Deciding to walk the path of personal development will be the most important decision of your life; it will provide the most challenges, but also the most rewards. There are many ways to work on your personal development. Some find individual or group counselling useful, others use coaching, yoga practice, spiritual practice, reading material from Elaine Aron, Brene Brown, M Scott Peck to name but a few (there are so many authors who write about personal growth). You can try philosophy courses, assertiveness courses, fitness challenges and much more.

So, are you ready to stand up to your full height? If you are not sure, talk to a friend or counsellor about it and discuss what you might need to put in place in order to pursue the path to maturity as an HSP. Without this maturity, you will not be functioning at your best, and the world will miss out.

At the end of the day, high sensitivity is an invitation
– an invitation to live your own precious and
fleeting life with genuine depth and intensity.
— TOM FALKENSTEIN

3

LET GO OF DEEPLY HELD FALSE BELIEF

It cannot be emphasised enough just how important it is to let go of deeply held false beliefs about yourself and the world. Much of what you believe will have been influenced by the attitudes of others as you grew up, so be aware that you might need to examine what you think and feel, to see if these things are *true*, *necessary* or *helpful*. For example, if you grew up as a sensitive person being told that you cry 'unnecessarily' or 'think too much', you will need to critically evaluate whether these generalised statements were ever true or if they were based on a misunderstanding of your sensitivity and your situation. One of the most common things that HSPs learn to let go of is the belief that they are inherently 'broken' or 'weak' somehow compared to others. If that is something that any part of you believes, give some consideration as to whether that was ever so.

Life for a sensitive person in a world made for the other 80% is actually much harder to navigate, so we often don't realise we are already inherently tough to have got this far. If you have been wounded or developed any kind of unhelpful behaviour as a response to the judgments of others during your upbringing or education, be prepared not only to change your mind, but also to grieve the loss of the stories that underpinned your understanding of yourself. Why? Because even if those stories were negative or untrue, at least for a time, they gave you an identity. Even negative things give us a sense of security, and when we change the basis of what we believe about ourselves, it can leave us feeling destabilised for a while, as we wait for something more true and positive to fill that space.

Be aware that, in being negatively judged by the majority, we can unintentionally become judgemental of them. Once we realise we are different, it is possible to see them as 'other' and to allow ourselves to devalue what they bring to the world. Try not to do that in the process of finding yourself; we need both HSPs and non-HSPs to bring their differing gifts in order for the world to function. Just don't let them overpower your sensitivity; they need it, whether they recognise it or not. *Respect yourself, respect them and respect your path.*

Give yourself time. All our beliefs about ourselves and others impact our life and the way we live it. Changing your view of yourself takes time, so make sure you allow yourself the time and resources for this important work. The great thing about letting go of false beliefs is that this not only makes space for new beliefs but also prepares you to deal with reality, and that reality, especially in relation to what you have to offer, might be surprisingly positive and hopeful.

4

STOP APOLOGISING

*P*lease stop apologising. When the world reflects to us that we are 'broken' or that something is the matter with us, we can get into the habit of apologising for our natural way of being; in some cases, we could even feel we have to apologise for existing. This habit of apologising, whilst it was useful in perhaps curtailing criticism or the disappointments and misunderstanding of others, is not going to serve you if you are apologising for your innate sensitive nature. You are genetically programmed to be highly sensitive and without highly sensitive people, the human race would not function and probably not exist, so feel free to take your place in this world without apology. This, of course, does not mean that we should stop considering others' feelings, or ways in which we may impact them – but there really is no apology needed for being sensitive per se – and especially don't apologise for being a mature sensitive person. Your self-awareness makes you invaluable to those around you in many ways, especially when you use your abilities in a supportive, mature way.

Let yourself be you – just like the rest of nature.

5

STOP COMPARING

'Comparison-itis' is a very destructive habit that HSPs often present with. As we grow up, we might hear others say, 'Why do you do that?', 'Why do you think that?', 'Can't you just do it like us?' People who make up the majority of the population are so used to being the same as each other that they might not understand why you might need different things, or why you might do things or experience things differently, or why you might value different things. They may have become exasperated with you or even formed the idea that you are somehow 'one down' or plain weird. When people respond to us like this, it can start an unhelpful habit of 'comparison-itis', whereby whatever we do, the choices we make, the way we feel, become something that we are compelled to compare to the other 80% and the way they do things, or how they feel about it, to check if we are 'doing it right'. We can start to assume that doing something differently or needing anything different means we are weak or 'just not doing it right'. This can lead to us doing life the non-HSP way, hoping that it will get easier if we just keep going. *But it doesn't, in fact, get easier, does it?*

There are many times when HSPs join in events, see everyone else enjoying themselves, whilst they themselves are feeling overloaded and just not comfortable at all. They put on a brave face nevertheless, and 'stick it out' or 'suck it up'. HSPs can spend a lot of time looking at others and themselves, trying to find out what is 'wrong' with them. Comparing in this way leads to 'what's wrong with me?' This then leads on to feeling broken, or that there is something the matter with us. 'Comparison-itis' can put a terrible strain on our nervous system and our self-worth. We might also force ourselves to do what everyone else is doing, without reaping the rewards that they do, maybe even burning out in the process.

'Comparison-itis' can therefore impact or colour very important decisions, for example:

- If or when to go into further education
- What type of work you 'should' do
- How many hours you 'should' work
- What kind of salary you 'should' accept in order to feel 'successful'
- Whether to take on a big mortgage
- How many friends you 'should' have
- What kind of partner you 'should' choose
- What car you 'should' drive
- What you 'should' provide for your children
- How much sleep you 'should' allow yourself

If you find yourself comparing, just check whether this is actually helping you, or if you are allowing it to force you to ignore your difference (and most probably your natural needs and gifts).

Stay healthy, stop comparing, be yourself, *choose what is authentic for you and take pride in that.*

6

PRACTISE A TYPE OF ASSERTIVENESS THAT MATCHES YOUR HSP NEEDS

Assertiveness consists of being able to ask for or get what you need whilst also being mindful of others' needs. It is different to aggression and passivity. Finding the middle ground, whilst also being assertive in a way that matches who you are, can be difficult at times. Remember that sometimes we can be in a habit of using hints and a quiet voice when asking for what we need. We can also be hyper-focussed on others' needs and let this drown out our own. Other HSPs might hear you very well when you ask for what you need, but the other 80% cannot always hear you and they appreciate clarity. Elaine Aron encourages HSPs to slightly raise their 'volume' when discussing things with the other 80%. That volume is not necessarily about the volume of the sound of your voice, it might be about the volume of your intent and clarity.

If you have a habit of overapologising, this could

potentially make it hard for your assertiveness to flourish. It is important to remember that the other person's response is their business, not yours. *Provided you practise respect and politeness with others, there is nothing wrong with asking for what you need.* When you are assertive, this does not mean that there is any sense of entitlement; sometimes the answer might be 'no'. An assertive person might check if there is a way to compromise, to make it more likely they will get what they want, but if at the end of that discussion the answer is still no, then this means you will need to use your creativity to try to find other ways to meet your needs. *What matters here is that you value your own needs as much as other people's.* If you have grown up having your natural sensitive needs reflected back to you as 'too much' or 'silly', then you will find it a little harder than others to ask for what you really need, perhaps almost trying to avoid needing anything because of the bad feelings you get when others do not respond helpfully.

On the path to HSP maturity, you will be starting to question false beliefs about your right to be you and, as a consequence, *your general assertiveness will rise.* One of the things you need to be aware of is the 'pendulum swing' of attempts at assertiveness. If you imagine a pendulum over at one side of its arc, say, the passive end, then when you let go and change, initially you might swing right over to the aggressive side in an attempt to increase your assertiveness skills. Be aware of this. The idea is to end up in the middle somewhere, effectively where assertiveness lies. Try not to beat yourself up if you get it wrong at first. That initial energy for change might come from a lot of built-up anger or desperation – an essential fuel for change at the beginning – just don't let it rule your trajectory or spoil the outcome. You can also take classes or enter counselling in order to learn and practise assertiveness skills and to have some support for any fears or challenges that happen along the way. Start with something small and gradually build up. Write things down if necessary and if at first you don't succeed, try again; you will find with time it does get easier. And when you start to get what you need, your life will start to improve on many levels; your inner strength will increase and you will feel calmer generally when asking for what you need.

Whilst you are practising, recognise that you might take quite a lot of swings at the ball before you manage a hit.

Recognizing what stresses us and not allowing it to do damage means seeing ourselves as a separate self from others. This defines your personal boundary.
— BARRIE JAEGER

7

HONOUR AND MANAGE YOUR EMOTIONS RESPECTFULLY AND WITH LOVE

*O*ne of the most precious gifts we have as HSPs is the intensity and agility with which our emotions present themselves. We are highly responsive to emotional cues and often have an emotionally based and intelligent response to situations that others miss due to their not always seeing the whole or the bigger picture.

Carl Jung, in 1913, said, 'Events bound up with powerful impressions can never pass off without leaving some trace on sensitive people.'

In order to honour your feelings, you have to take them seriously. The compassion you have for others has to be applied equally to yourself. Part of this process is addressing any false beliefs you might have about your emotions.

If you have grown up believing that your emotional sensitivity is a sign of weakness, you might need to talk about this with your counsellor. There is no such thing as a 'wrong' emotion. Emotions are signallers about situations; they are information; they help us and drive us to see a situation for what it is. We identify a need and then we can find ways to meet that need. For example, if you have moved to a new town and your friends are far away, you might find yourself feeling sad and isolated. The sadness is telling you that you are in need of connection. It is not a weakness to feel sad, and it's not exactly emotionally intelligent to ignore sadness and suffer. If you listen to your emotion, you will acknowledge that you are in need of connection, then you can put in place the actions that will help you to connect with new people or reconnect with friends far away. The role of feelings like this as signallers are not just for you either. Sensitive people signal to others about situations that matter for the group, things that the other 80% might be too busy to notice. It is important to love your ability to feel emotions so intensely, because they are a gift not only to you, but to the world. Be non-judgmental about your feelings; treat them as handy hints that have the potential to influence your actions and decisions positively. In fact, it may well be your ability to feel positive feelings like love and awe, to be moved by sad situations, and your emotional awareness of others' feelings, that attracts people to you.

An important thing about empathy in HSPs is that your innate sensitivity makes you stronger in *cognitive empathy*. This is not just empathy where you feel someone else's feelings as if by osmosis, or you know how they feel because you have felt it yourself. It is about the ability to imagine how someone else is feeling, to imagine a situation from their point of view, whilst still being able to see other points of view (including yours) at the same time. It is about the skill of being able to *think* about feelings. It is this skill that allows HSPs in particular to be quick to understand another person and to navigate social, tactical and interpersonal situations with effectiveness and compassion. This is an ability that not everyone has innately and it is a reason why sometimes you might find yourself able to understand and respond appropriately to a situation, whilst others might struggle.

Never underestimate this cognitive empathic ability, it underpins deep connections and wisdom. It supports our emotional compass to create meaningful and authentic bonds and to make wise decisions, not only on our own behalf, but on behalf of others.

*Emotions are the harmonics of the soul and the
compass of the heart.*

8

THE BIND OF HIGH SENSITIVITY: DEPRESSION AND ANXIETY VS AUTHENTICITY

ighly sensitive people (HSPs) are sought after nowadays for their creativity, attention to detail, reliability, emotional depth and responsiveness, value compass and interpersonal skills, amongst other things. Even so, as a minority en route to success, they may struggle with anxiety, depression or their search for personal authenticity in a world that sometimes feels foreign to them. Here is a list of some of those struggles and the kind of work that will help to put down authentic roots underpinning a life with direction, meaning and personal happiness. Highly sensitive people have some of the toughest struggles but often surmount them with aplomb once they recognise they are not alone and that this is a journey that excludes no one.

Two of the things that might be at the root of feelings of anxiety or depression for HSPs:

- We struggle to match ourselves to what appears to be 'normal' in the dominant culture and deplete ourselves in the process. For example, long working hours might be a struggle, or we feel more affected by the ups and downs of life or the attitudes of those around us. In short, life seems so much more stressful for us and when we come into conflict with societal norms, we might struggle with a sense of shame or hopelessness, or a fear of 'getting it wrong'. We don't really know who we are.

- Or, we know who we are inside, but struggle to express our true selves on the outside, causing confusion and stress to ourselves and those who come into contact with us. We find ourselves living a half-life, experiencing more dissatisfaction than most and experiencing less of the intense natural highs that a sensitive person is capable of. We struggle to know how we might change that situation or even to believe that perhaps we should change it.

Both of the situations above are common in HSPs who are struggling and they create a bind that can keep us stuck, but they need not be permanent. If change is possible, what might get in the way?

- We may have learnt habits from the dominant culture that are getting in the way of our authentic being.

- We may harbour beliefs that are not accurate, about ourselves and what we can expect.

- We may be retelling ourselves the old stories of our life and projecting those forward rather than reinventing our story. Or reliving old wounds out of habit that distract us from moving forward.
- We may lack patience with ourselves in making the changes that will help us to feel better or deny ourselves the resources that will help those changes to happen.
- We may not be willing to accept who we are and want to be like the other 80%.
- We may not be valuing the beauty of our trait and valuing the approval of the majority more than authenticity.
- We may have developed short-term cultural thinking, expecting that life-changing work can happen overnight.
- We may be intolerant of the natural losses that go with growth.
- We may not have set up a network of support, professional or otherwise, or the companionship of other HSPs.
- We may be avoiding the work of dealing with past wounds that are holding us back.
- We may be trapped in 'sunk cost' thinking, 'I've invested so much time and energy in this that I would rather carry on being less happy than feel like I "wasted" my time.'
- We have not yet thought through what we wish our true purpose to be, so we remain uninspired and small in our view or our role in life.

- We may have bought into the modern-day habit of 'skipping' around social media, picking up headlines and not reading more deeply, thus depriving ourselves of the intellectual and spiritual nutrition and critical thinking that helps to build HSP wisdom and confidence.

What can we do now that might help to turn around feelings of anxiety and depression?

- Read more about your temperament trait of high sensitivity.
- Converse with other highly sensitive people to help create a sense of community and support.
- Put professional support in place if this is what you need, invest in yourself and your future. Choose someone who is HSP-aware and able to walk alongside you on the longer, more winding path.
- Make a commitment to deal with wounds to your heart or soul that are long overdue for healing.
- Start to think about what you have to offer that is complementary to the dominant culture, yet authentically you.
- Think about what spirituality or connectedness means to you and spend more time in nature to hasten this sense of wonder and belonging.
- Start making longer-term plans to live a more authentic life and reduce your impatience with yourself and your path. Precious things take time.
- Think about what your values are and begin to

check your decisions against these values, even the small ones.

- Remember that potential for change can happen every five minutes. Ask yourself 'what would I be doing right now if I were mindful of what makes me happy and myself as a highly sensitive person?'

For those who are already taking charge of their HSP needs, what have you found so far that is helpful and confidence-building on this journey?

9

LEARN TO LOVE YOUR
DIFFERENCE

All living beings have an underlying response to difference or 'otherness'. The initial response is one based on survival. Being cautious about something different is a protective response that has been present through evolutionary history. Notice how our pets respond in new situations. It makes sense that they are initially cautious. The reaction is based on an innate checking system to see if the other person or thing is a threat.

On a deep level, and often unconsciously, human beings become suspicious of difference, whether it is visual, cultural or something else. That threat could be instant danger of death, or it could be potential threat to resources, land space, health, dignity, etc. Living things compete with each other for resources and often come into conflict over these. One only has to see the way in which whole countries or even next-door neighbours can become enemies, to see that difference, misunderstanding and fear of threat or loss are age-old issues that can get out of control. *So when we notice how we ourselves are different, we need to be aware of not seeing that as a threat but also understand how our difference might initially make others cautious.*

Applying this knowledge to ourselves as HSPs can be useful, because, in fact, we sometimes even see an aspect of ourselves as 'unwelcome' or a threat. We could potentially see the other 80% as a threat. Many HSPs see their own difference as sensitive people as a threat within themselves. They might try to deal with this by working to act and behave like the other 80%, or they might berate themselves for not being something else or 'like the others'. HSPs might develop issues around self-trust because of this difficulty accepting their own difference.

Learning to love your difference requires deep reflection and intelligence. It means overcoming fear and prejudices about your natural trait by studying it, making friends with it and letting go of unhelpful false beliefs about what it is and what it is not. The same thing happens when we as humans overcome prejudices in the world; we are less likely to regard others with suspicion if we get to know them, if we learn about their gifts, respect their needs and appreciate their differences. *The way to overcome the barriers of difference is to develop stronger empathy, a resource that HSPs usually have in abundance.*

Learning to love your difference is part of becoming a mature HSP. Sensitive people have many good qualities and we provide much to others in the form of compassion, creativity, wisdom, foresight and emotional responsiveness. *Let's not devalue our beautiful trait in a fit of shame, just because we are unique in the way we experience the world.*

We all have different capacities and different roles
in this world.
(*ANONYMOUS HSP*)

It is likely that your difference will be something that will complement and add to your life or that of those around you. HSPs are good at seeing opportunities for harmony and creative solutions. By encouraging safety and cooperation within different groups, we can help everyone to live a better-resourced life. But first, we need to know and trust ourselves to be safe, friendly and generous, then we can help others to see us that way too.

*Every living thing is different in some way. Let your deep
emotional colours become part of the magnificent rainbow of life.*

10

LEARN FACTUAL DETAILS ABOUT YOUR TRAIT

I have met so many HSPs who are truly suffering simply because they have no factual information about their natural trait and how to take care of or understand themselves. In order to live our lives fully, we need to understand what makes us tick, what we need and the kinds of activities and environments that are health-giving for us. We need to understand that we do not have a 'condition', a 'processing disorder' or anything else that undermines our ability to thrive. Elaine Aron, PhD's research and her books are an enormous help in understanding what the HSP trait of sensory processing sensitivity is, and what it is not. Her books also give us a complete reframe of why this matters and what our place is in the world.

Learn some simple facts about highly sensitive people. For example, if you are suffering with tiredness but you don't know that HSPs need a couple more hours of rest or sleep than the other 80%, how would you be in a position to reorganise your sleep patterns? If you do not realise that

HSPs' nervous systems work faster and more intensely than the other 80%, then you might interpret the fact that you appear to 'startle easily' as being fearful, rather than that you have intensely responsive reflexes. Factual information helps us to interpret the basics of who we are, what we need and to find what makes us happy. A wise and mature HSP understands this and is familiar with the nuts and bolts of what makes us highly sensitive; this leads to clarity, acceptance and optimism about how we will fit in and respond to the world. If you have not done so already, take a look at the chapter in this book on the facts about our trait.

Please, please, take time to read not only books or research papers on high sensitivity, but books that help you to understand yourself and develop a philosophy. Use caution when choosing reading material; check that any stated facts resonate with common sense and good-quality research. Reading should be a life-long pursuit. Without studying the wisdom of others, you will find it very difficult to hone your own natural wisdom, to find a context for your response to the world and let it serve you and your community. Reading takes time, effort and patience, but it is something that all self-respecting HSPs will do as part of their education, daily growth and self-care. Make friends with books (and audiobooks).

I'd always felt like I didn't belong, my interpretation
of the world seemed different from everyone.
Learning about this trait taught me that I'm not all
that different, it's just my experience that's different.
(*ANONYMOUS HSP*)

11

KNOW YOUR DEEPLY HELD VALUES AND ASSIMILATE THEM

K nowing and understanding the values that underpin your response to the world will open up some clarity as you make decisions in your life. Life coaches, especially those who are HSP-aware, are particularly good at this process and identifying your top three values will very much act as a rudder in giving your life direction.

Look back on decisions you have made and ask yourself what was behind that particular decision; what factors were you considering (perhaps that others were not so concerned about). Did you fully go with your values, or did you end up trying to harness your values to those of others in the decision process, perhaps ending up with a result that did not quite work out the way you wished? These factors will help you to identify the values that underpin your view of life and any innate temperament or personal qualities that operate when you are choosing your direction. Every decision we make will have some underlying value attached and as we mature, we become more grounded and able to sense which way our rudder wants us to go.

Although HSPs come in all shapes and sizes, unsurprisingly, their values are often similar, so this might be an opportunity to talk to any HSP friends and discuss what kinds of values matter for highly sensitive people, then consider what kinds of roles those values might make them especially suitable for. Values are part of the map of life for everyone, but especially HSPs because they are very strong motivators for us.

I have learned that as long as I hold fast to my beliefs and values – and follow my own moral compass – then the only expectations I need to live up to are my own.

— MICHELLE OBAMA

12

THE PROCESS OF CHANGE, THE STAGES, THE CHALLENGES

In order to achieve maturity as an HSP, it is necessary to accept change. Change is not a choice; it bears down on us, sometimes like an unwelcome guest, sometimes as the hero we have been waiting a long time for. Understanding the *process* of change will help you to identify your own process in the journey towards HSP maturity. The stages of the process flow as follows: *pre-contemplation, contemplation, preparation, action,* and *maintenance.* You can find yourself going to and fro along this process at times, but if you understand how change works, you will be more supportive and compassionate about your own process, and you will also have a guide to what is the next step for you.

In *pre-contemplation*, we are mostly unaware that we even need to make any changes; we are blissfully ignorant that there is another way. We might be suffering but imagining that this is just how life is, or we might be resisting offers of change because of firmly held false beliefs we hold. The *contemplation* phase is a stage that happens when we are either confronted, pushed or invited into thinking about our life. Maybe we have been anxious or depressed for some time, maybe we have burnt out at work, maybe we have issues with low self-worth or anger; we may have developed an illness that is made worse by stress, or we might be incredibly and depressingly bored. Any of these might lead us to want to work on our personal development, to make changes.

During the *contemplation* stage, we are thinking about what might need to change and why. This is followed by the *preparation* stage, when we start to plan how those changes will be made. This planning might be done alone, or we might perhaps go into counselling or coaching to look at what steps might be needed: when and how. For example, if your work or career is causing you to become ill, you might do some research, take some tests to see what suits you best and so on. You might also think about how many hours per week are suitable for you; how you might manage financial change. Perhaps you will contemplate how you plan your work-life balance, who you might like to have around you as supporters, perhaps even creating a weekly activity plan that gives you time for work, rest and play.

Once the preparation is done, you will be ready to take action that will bring you closer to a more authentic and healthy HSP life. The *action* stage will also need support; change is hard, even if it brings benefits. It can also be beneficial to change one small thing at a time before you attempt the bigger issues. Build your confidence first and aim to develop patience. You might need to deal with others who are not used to these changes or deal with a sense of loss as you let go of what did not work for you – relationships, friendships, ways of being, lifestyle choices, unhelpful expectations, commitments – you might need time to grieve. Grieving is natural; it is a process and good for us. It is a time of acknowledgement of loss, honouring what was and moving towards what lies ahead. Even though grieving might sound difficult to you, please make time for it; every experience of your life has moved you to this point, it is important to honour these things with time and attention so as to experience gratitude for what was good and to allow the weight of sadness or regret to pass. You can then welcome the future with renewed openness and energy.

Once your actions start to become more of an everyday positive and natural way of being, you will move into the *maintenance* stage. It can seem like this is a place to take it easy, but no, this is a very important stage, because you will need to use new ways to deal with unexpected stressors or unexpected gifts, and you will need to review and re-examine your plans to make sure they are fit for purpose on a regular basis. Life changes, so the plan that works this year might not work as well next year.

As HSPs, we work through a number of issues as we proceed towards authenticity and these manifest in a variety of outward signs in terms of our attitude to our natural trait and the world we live in. Jacquelyn Strickland's adapted *Stages of cultural awareness for HSPs* is a good example of what kinds of outward signs we exhibit depending on where we are at in our HSP development.

Whatever the reason for you to be reading this book, it is likely that some part of you wants life to be different on some level. The fact that you are reading it means you are at least in the contemplative stage and possibly in the planning stage, so remember to give yourself a pat on the back for getting this far.

> I understand why I need to back away from society and find my own peaceful places. [The hardest skill to learn] has been to stop and be still.
> (ANONYMOUS HSP)

13

SEE HOW YOUR TRAIT PREPARES YOU TO BE YOUR BEST

It is easy to forget, when you are navigating life out there in the non-HSP world, that there is a reason for you to be different, and your success and your definition of success will also be different to the majority. Familiarise yourself with the positives of our trait, so that you can align yourself with the best of yourself as a highly sensitive person. Here are some of the things we are particularly good at:

- Listening deeply and understanding others.
- Paying attention to subtle or small details that reveal more about situations that others simply do not notice.
- We are highly conscientious.
- We are benign, compassionate and intelligent leaders, rarely seeking power over others, preferring to share power.

- We are highly adaptable (much as others might be surprised).
- We are adept at finding ways to work with new situations and we are highly creative in doing so.
- We tend to be highly creative, appreciative of the arts and eloquent both verbally and in the written word. Our understanding of the world and how it works is very much in touch with reality, even when it goes against our values. For this reason, it is important not to stay quiet, and to find ways of sharing our thoughts, our wisdom and our take on what is happening around us.
- We are highly attuned to our environment and other people. This means our capacity to have good relationships, to observe what is happening around us and to parent our children is of a high quality. We make excellent medics, teachers, nurturers and specialists because of this special attunement and understanding of others.
- We come in all shapes and sizes and all different personality types, so we can offer a wide range of skills and understanding to multiple organisations, roles and activities.
- We would naturally take the long, winding road, rather than rush into decisions or actions that could have major unhelpful consequences, so we can be relied upon to make thoroughly thought-through decisions that take the whole picture into account. (Imagine what minds like that could do to planetary environmentalism, public education,

national health resources, conflict resolution and politics.)

- Due to our deep and constant processing, we can be great to have around for conversation.
- In an emergency, since we have often contemplated the what-ifs, we can be looked to for urgent direction. For example, we are the most likely to have checked where the fire exits are on entering the theatre and so on.
- We have excellent predictive skills and can foresee both problems and possibilities that others often miss. We encompass longer-term planning with ease.

You might be able to add something more to the list.

The above are only a few of the things we can offer, but how often do we fail to show up with confidence in these skills? And sometimes, do we fail to show up where we are needed because we think we are not welcome? If we don't show up with our authentic skill set, this could be the worst disservice we could do, both to ourselves and those who need our perspective. Unless we talk about our skills, even our employers might not be able to appreciate them.

> ...Though some HSPs may be in the consultation room where decisions are made, there are not nearly enough.

> ...Pretty much every other skill is given language and a pay point on a performance-development

review, but sensitivity is not, even though in many
cases it is essential for the role.

— *HANNAH JANE WALKER*

14

ATTEND TO YOUR SPIRITUAL JOURNEY

*E*ven though many HSPs are not religious or following a particular spiritual practice, they are nevertheless often spiritual people. Elaine Aron says we are the types of people that often held the role in the past of 'priestly advisor'. These advisors can come in all shapes and sizes, from wise, old aunts to shamans that were supported in the community for their wisdom and intellectual resources. We have a sense of connection to things bigger than ourselves; we have a connection to 'the numinous'.

With this in mind, think about yourself in the context of a spiritual journey, especially how that journey is influenced by your degree of maturity as an HSP. All the things you will learn in this book will help develop that sense of spiritual connection to our planet, other human beings and to something bigger. HSPs who neglect this part of the journey toward maturity will find themselves feeling like a piece of the puzzle is missing. Elaine Aron's articles on the 'numinous' might be a good place to learn more about this way of being. A regular practice to maintain connection with our spiritual self is essential to underpin the direction of our life's journey.

> You have to grow from the inside out. None can teach you, none can make you spiritual. There is no other teacher but your own soul.
> – Swami Vivekananda

15

RECOGNISE YOUR RESPONSE TO CRITICISM AND YOUR OWN SELF-JUDGMENT, LETTING GO OF OTHERS' OPINIONS

HSPs naturally experience intense or deep emotions – and this includes our experience of shame. Often, HSPs have been shamed for their natural response to situations. They also have an innate strategy of liking to 'do it once and do it right'. This level of conscientiousness ensures we do reasonably well in manifesting acceptable behaviour and contributions, but remember that, despite wanting to get things right, occasionally and inevitably, we will get it wrong. If our strategy of thinking things through, observing and taking time to make decisions has worked well for us, there is a possibility that we may get used to always getting it right, meaning when we get it wrong, it could feel more devastating than necessary, simply because getting it wrong doesn't happen often. In this circumstance, we need to find a way to take criticism as information, not a judgement about our whole selves as a person.

Being thoughtful creatures, we will be careful not to upset others, but if, for example, we find we have accidentally created a problem for someone, it will be important to apologise and move on, rather than continue to beat ourselves up for 'getting it wrong'. We are not super-beings that have less right to make mistakes than anyone else. Forgiving ourselves for mistakes will make sure we do not waste our valuable energy dismantling our self-esteem and will instead give us time to examine ways to improve. The thing that often troubles HSPs is finding a way to move on after a criticism, something the other 80% find a lot easier. If you have a particular difficulty with this, it would be well worth it to consult a counsellor to find out how, perhaps, old wounds, experiences and firmly held false beliefs are playing out in your response and prolonging painful feelings or negative self-image. It is hard to escape a trap that exists in our own minds. Along with this, develop strong self-compassion and forgiveness; offer to yourself what you offer to everyone else.

There is no failure, only feedback.
— ROBERT ALLEN

16

GET BETTER AT ASSESSING PEOPLE, WHAT THEY SAY, WHAT THEY THINK, THEIR INFLUENCE ON YOU. HOW TO IGNORE 'SHOULDS' AND 'OUGHTS' THAT DON'T BELONG

A mature sensitive person recognises that there can be a difference between others' opinions of us and the reality. We can only know the reality if we know and accept ourselves with compassion and clarity. Others can only comment on what they see, and they will interpret this according to their own version of what is good and bad, what is right and wrong, and how they experience the world. Since we are different to the majority, it can be helpful to recognise that their experience, and their version of what is 'normal', can vary greatly to ours. If we have been unduly criticised in childhood, or held to impossible standards, those wounds might have an impact on how we handle comments from others. Karen Horney's work on 'the tyranny of the shoulds' speaks to the importance of examining our self-talk. Our experiences growing up may also have had an impact on our choice of friends, partners and colleagues. It can take a while for us to let go of habits like accepting people's opinions at face value or depending on others' opinions in order to feel good about ourselves.

Remember to give yourself time to assess how much attention to give the opinions of others and the messages that you receive from the media. The media generally repeats the ideas of the majority, or what is popular in the moment, yet as a minority, those ideas might not resonate with us. Keeping friends around us who demean sensitivity, or persistently disrespect difference, is a sure way to deplete our energy and slow down our progress to maturity. What matters is to critically evaluate what we hear and what we read, to ensure that what we learn fits with an up to date and growing version of our values and selfhood. Stay open-minded, kind and compassionate with people, but diligent in moderating the impact of opinions that are not informed. I heard a wise person once say, 'Do not blithely accept the opinion of anyone to whom you would not go for advice.'

Inevitably, as we mature, due to our deep processing and sensitivity to subtleties, we often reach the goal of understanding what underlies people's motives and actions before they do. As a result, we might find that we need patience and compassion for others as well as ourselves in those moments. Just because we understand someone and feel for them, however, should not stop us looking after our own interests when it matters.

Reading others is an energy-consuming activity that HSPs are good at. However, there are shortfalls if we have grown up mistrusting our own judgement. If our younger life has been full of trauma or unresolved conflict, we will often associate certain moods, emotions or actions with meanings that fit that situation long ago. As adults, it takes practice to develop the ability to use our powerful analytical mind to be aware of others *in the present context*. Our intuitive ability to attune to others is another gift, and yet, this also needs to be used wisely, in case our empathy causes us to adopt a role with someone that is not going to work in our best interests. Intuition needs monitoring and awareness to be effective. One of the most helpful things I learnt was to remember that what people do is more important than what they say. Truth is in actions. In the process of finding truth, we need to take into account our own wounds and bias and give ourselves time to think about our intuitions. Be prepared to be wrong sometimes, but also remember when you were right, so as to honour your gift of perception and use it wisely on your own behalf and on behalf of others.

Additionally, be aware if you have developed an aversion to conflict. It is possible to learn how to deal with difference that arises without it becoming stuck or harmful. Conflict resolution skills are teachable, so do look for ways to learn these skills to help you move forward with your plans for HSP maturity.

Peace is not the absence of conflict, but the presence of creative alternatives for responding to conflict.

– Dorothy Thompson

17

CHOOSING BETTER FRIENDS

A good friend is someone whose company you enjoy and with whom you have formed a mutually satisfying relationship that is both relaxed, meaningful and worth any effort you put in. Someone does not have to be exactly like you in order to be considered a friend. In fact, that might be a great advantage; and, of course, they will not be perfect and neither will you. A friend will care about you, but both you and they know that, ultimately, you are each responsible only for yourselves and your own happiness. Overall, they will have most of the qualities below. A friend is someone who:

- Likes you for who you are.
- Supports you in pursuing what makes you happy.
- Will tell you if they are worried about you.
- Is not afraid to disagree with you.
- Will deliver home truths on the rare occasions when you really need them.
- Does not tell you what to do but will offer an opinion if asked.

- Is respectful, truthful, kind and fair in their dealings with you.
- Has good boundaries and will not offer something to you that they cannot afford to give, in material things or in terms of time.
- Will not demand something of you that might harm you.
- Gives you a listening ear when you need it whilst taking care to be balanced about the amount of support you give each other.
- Is honest and reliable in things that matter.
- Even if they don't understand, they will still be understanding.
- Is fun to be with and has a good sense of humour.
- Is capable of discussing problems between you and apologising when appropriate.
- Will take into account your sensitive nature and appreciate you for it, even if they are not highly sensitive themselves.
- Would never interfere with your other friendships.
- Will be themselves around you.
- Will respect your secrets, your home and your belongings.

If you have friends who are a drain, or who really do not seem to know or respect who you are, or your sensitivity and personal choices, think about how much time you wish to give them.

Importantly, the above list is also useful for checking whether you are a good enough friend to others.

The only reward of virtue is virtue; the only way to have a friend is to be one.

— RALPH WALDO EMERSON

18

OBSERVING AND ENFORCING HEALTHY BOUNDARIES

A personal boundary is something that sets a limit to what you will accept from or offer others. However, *boundaries mean nothing if they are not recognised or observed by you or by others.* Boundaries are central to our self-worth and offer protection from overwhelm. Some HSPs struggle with boundaries, sometimes due to feeling unable to say what they want, or sometimes because they find it hard not to respond to others' demands or needs since they feel them so strongly. The attunement or empathy you feel for another human being is a particular gift, but if it constantly leads you to try to make things right for another person, this can leave you open to exhaustion or manipulation that is not good for you. In order to work on this, it is important to work out what your own reasonable boundaries actually are. For example, do you need uninterrupted time to work or rest? Do you need others to respect your things if they borrow them? Do you need others to respect your privacy? Do you need to babysit your neighbour's kids less often? Do you need to be mindful not to work too many hours? These are just a few of the boundaries we could think about.

A boundary sensitive people need to be particularly aware of is around violence, fear and force. *Due to their differential susceptibility, HSPs are more deeply traumatised by bullying, abusive or violent behaviour or careless handling.* Our nervous system processes pain and shock very intensely. So make sure you have a respectful zero tolerance of this, especially if someone lays hands aggressively on you, and even if they say you are 'overreacting' or 'it wasn't so bad'. Your body and emotions will tell you the truth. If you know someone is prone to being too rough and doesn't take a hint, it might be best to avoid them in the future.

Once you know what your important boundaries are, you can think about ways in which to communicate those boundaries. After all, other people are not mind readers, so they often need clear, calm information rather than hints. This is particularly true of the other 80% who do not observe your responses to situations as keenly as you do theirs. It is not helpful to put up with something that is crossing boundaries for so long that you eventually blow up; fear of upsetting others can bring this about, but inevitably it will upset them if you inform them of your exasperation and boundary information like an exploding volcano. It can also be useful to ask others about their limits and boundaries, to clarify what is acceptable, or what is important to them. For example, what does 'OK, just a little while' mean to them?

In order to practise maintaining healthy boundaries, you might need also to increase your level of confidence and communication skills. If you have a particular issue with self-confidence or shyness, it might be a good idea to attend therapy so that you can not only understand where your difficulties might be coming from but also get a chance to role-play saying 'no'. Therapy might also provide an opportunity to practise some delaying techniques that will help you to take time to work out what you wish to say, especially if someone is asking something from you that you are not sure you can give without a lot of disruption or fatigue. Doing too much for others is a common experience for HSPs, but a balance will return if you pursue a mature attitude towards your own and others' boundaries and resources.

Another way of developing better boundaries is to practise being more 'boundaried' *with yourself.* Do you find that it is hard to be consistent with your self-care, for example? Do you promise yourself a walk in the forest and then not take yourself there? Do you promise yourself to eat more healthy food or drink less alcohol and then not follow up? These are all opportunities to observe your process and to intervene to bring more HSP health and better boundaries to your life.

19

CREATE SPACES AND TIME TO COMMUNE WITH OTHER HSPS

This is an often-neglected area of HSP life. Other HSPs are good for us, especially those who are on a mindful path towards HSP self-awareness and maturity. We spend a lot of time mixing with the other 80%, and whilst that might also be a good thing, we do need time with our HSP friends to feel understood, encouraged and 'met' where we are.

Many HSPs describe a feeling of being 'lonely in a crowd', and I think this might be because we sense that others are not necessarily attuned to the things that we are, and they certainly don't 'get' us entirely, even though they might be appreciative of our trait. This situation can lead to a general sense of isolation or boredom that can really only be explained by being apart from your sensitive 'family'. Do take the time to find other HSPs who would like to spend some time doing something together, whether that is a walk in the forest, a conversation over a cup of tea, reading a book together in silence, or a group activity.

It cannot be underestimated how the energy of other HSPs re-energises and inspires. The ability to instantly 'go deep' is something that is common to HSPs; no time consuming small talk. The freedom to be sensitive, to have feelings, not to have to explain so much of your perspective or experience is both freeing and energising and helps your conversation to go beyond the superficial. Being with other HSPs will also help to remind you why you hold certain things dear, close to your heart: your values, your attitudes, your appreciation of nature, your spiritual life. All these things matter 'out there' and are something that you offer your community, but we all need to nurture our sensitive soul, and being with other HSPs helps to do that.

Spending time in nature with highly sensitive children can be a great source of grounding and connection, and they will greatly appreciate being in your company as a fellow sensitive soul.

20

PROCESSING THE GRIEF OF LETTING GO OF HABITS, ENVIRONMENTS, ACTIVITIES, BELIEFS AND PEOPLE THAT DON'T SERVE YOUR PATH TOWARDS WHOLENESS, INTEGRITY AND LOVE

The path to HSP maturity is sometimes arduous. When we first find out about high sensitivity, it is like a wonderful gift has landed on our doorstep; we welcome it with open arms and start to re-evaluate the way we view ourselves. Instead of thinking that we 'feel too much', we realise that we simply feel more intensely. Instead of feeling like a failure because we get tired more quickly, we realise that our very busy nervous system requires more rest time. All of these things help us to reframe our whole view of who we are.

An important part of the changes that happen when we get accurate information about our trait is to learn to let go of old habits, environments, activities, beliefs and people that no longer support our well-being. For example, perhaps we have a long-time friend who only seems to contact us when they want something and is not there for us when we need something from them. This friendship might be something we wish to move on from. Letting go not only involves identifying areas of our life that need adjusting, but we also have to prepare for the process of grief that is inevitable if we are going to let go of things that might have been present in our lives for decades. Sometimes, those things are ideas about ourselves, like realising we are not weak, we are in fact strong. The changing of our perspective on our relationship with work; for example, realising we are quality rather than quantity people and that standard forty-plus-hour working weeks are not optimal. Or we might realise that our sensitivity is the reason that extended periods of socialising can be tiring; we are friendly, but due to our intensity and awareness of subtleties, we have a limit to how much socialising we can do before we feel like we are burning out. This leads to needing to say 'no' to the number or type of social occasions we attend, or maybe the length of time we stay there. Again, there is grief, because the way we live in the world is a part of our identity and this starts to change when we find out that we are highly sensitive. Whilst so much makes sense, there is still a loss of the 'old' world we existed in. Donna Lancaster's book *The Bridge* covers the topic of grief very well.

For some of us, we may realise that there are one or more toxic relationships that do not work for us. Over the years, we may have thought we needed those relationships, or they may have helped to define who we are. But now that we know more about who we really are, those relationships no longer fit. The person who persuaded us to go clubbing the night before work might not be someone whom we can socialise with as much. The person who was so demanding of our time or depended so much on us emotionally without doing the same in return, might have to go. Maybe we got kudos by doing as much overtime as everyone else, and we felt good about that, but now we need to say 'no' so that we can get the rest we need. Maybe, without realising it, with a certain friendship group we drank more alcohol than necessary, either to impress others or to cope with the stress of living a life that did not match our sensitive needs. When we let go of old habits, initially it can leave a hole in our life that needs to be filled by something healthier. At first that can feel lonely or even boring, so there is a lot of adjustment involved in reaching maturity as an HSP.

Change and growing in maturity is not all hearts and flowers, some of it is sobbing into the pillow at night as we watch a lot of things we believed about ourselves disappear, leaving a question mark over the future. We may grieve the amount of hurt we experienced in our lives, we might feel sad, or angry, or numb. However we feel, it is important to honour the process of letting go and to nurture self-compassion for our growing pains.

One of the things you will need is an HSP friend or two, someone who understands, and maybe even a therapist who can help you not only to make the changes that will support your new life as a mature sensitive person, but also to mourn what you will let go of in order to achieve an authentic, sensitive life filled with integrity and love. Something I felt helped a lot in this process was to write an unsent letter to my previous self, the one that was hurt, found life so hard, suffered, struggled and made mistakes. In the letter, I honoured what had gone before, appreciated the efforts of my former self to survive, and made a promise for a better life in the future. The whole process was very therapeutic; you might find it helpful to try this, or other rituals, as a way of addressing the inevitable grief and future joys of changing your life.

21

PROCESSING AND HEALING PAST WOUNDS

*E*laine Aron talks about how important it is for HSPs to heal past wounds. Our trait means it is possible to sustain deeper wounds more easily than the other 80%. So when we begin the path towards HSP maturity, we face this process with a number of emotional wounds that need healing. For many HSPs, this healing will take place in a therapeutic environment; that respectful time and space will give us what we need as we explore our wounds, review how we want things to change and put better self-care in place. Many of our wounds have added complications since our suffering will have been interpreted to us by the dominant culture as some kind of weakness or failure to meet expectations. Having a non-judgmental atmosphere to look at those painful wounds and to reframe what happened to us is something that every HSP deserves. The good news is that due to our vantage sensitivity, we tend to do very well with interventions like therapy and often make faster progress than the other 80%. This is because we have depth of processing and can move very quickly in terms of our understanding of healing processes. This doesn't mean we can avoid feeling the hurt, but it does mean that we can make sense of things and see the bigger picture faster.

There is an exception to this: due to our deep nature, we also form particularly deep bonds with those we love, meaning when we lose them, it has a significantly more profound effect on our recovery. It may take us longer to process personal loss than others. Make the most of your sensitivity to help you work through what you need to do. You might also find it useful to use creativity, such as art, music, writing or drama, to work through your challenges; creativity comes naturally to HSPs, so don't waste it. Spending time in nature will also help a great deal with your healing, *never underestimate just how much that is so.*

Above all, remember that wounds take up a lot of space within you, and until you have begun to deal with them, you will find it hard to find the space within you for the self-understanding and feelings that make life joyful and rewarding.

Nature has its time and then lets go, preparing for renewal. Let your heart and soul grieve and heal in their own season, don't resist and don't force.

22

CREATE A PROTECTIVE LAYER, LET COMMENTS SLIP OFF

This is much easier said than done and is linked to how we view criticism and boundaries (see earlier chapters). *What makes the difference is your belief about what you hear.* People can say whatever they want, but it can only affect you negatively if you give what they say space and credence. If a part of yourself believes what people say about you, that is not their fault. It is your responsibility to examine your perception of yourself. You might need to attend to this in a therapeutic environment, or with a good friend, where you can challenge your thoughts and ideas about yourself. It's worth remembering that most of the other 80% have little understanding of our difference and they can only see us in comparison to themselves, so they will sometimes say things about us or to us that are outrageously inaccurate or misinformed without knowing it.

Sometimes what comes up for us is a highly emotional

response to what is being said. If this happens, it is OK to take time out to compose yourself. Whilst it can feel shameful to respond so emotionally to what others say or demand of you, *do remember that it is in your nature to have an intense emotional experience, whether positive or negative, so if you feel overwhelmed, take yourself away for reflection time.* If you can speak in the moment, simply say that you need some time to process what they are saying. Removing yourself now won't take away your right to come back to it later. You might even decide that regardless of the strength of your response, the situation, in retrospect, is not important enough to you to spend any further time talking about it. You may decide to 'let it slip off your protective coating'. The passing of time is a great means to higher perspective, so always give yourself time to think and reflect before responding.

One of the traps about people's judgment of us can be that we feel, in that moment, that we have to 'justify' ourselves. This happens when the other person seems to demand an immediate justification or response to what they are asking or have said. Or they may choose to say it in public, where we feel we have to 'save face'. It is their business if they expect a response to a negative or unhelpful statement or question, but it is entirely your choice whether or not to cooperate in your destruction by answering without thinking things through.

There are any number of ways to respond in this situation, and you can explore these when you have time, but some of the main ways you can respond are:

- You can choose to stay quiet and simply ignore it.

- You can choose to say you will think about what they said and come back to them.
- If you feel they are severely crossing a boundary, you can say, 'that statement does not deserve a response', or, 'what a strange thing to say' and walk away.

No one can force you to stay in a conversation that is destructive. If you give yourself time to think before responding, you might discover that what that person believes is nothing to do with you.

However, if, after reflecting, you believe something they said makes sense or might be true, take it to a safe space like therapy or to a trusted friend, where you can unpack it honestly and receive the support you need. Through this processing, you will be able to find ways to heal from any sustained wounds, or you might discover that they have a point and decide to work on that.

HSPs are defined by their deep processing, so when confronted with something uncomfortable, honour that gift by giving yourself time to process those words or ideas. We are not built like the other 80%, *we are not meant to act impulsively*, so stay true to your real self and take your time. You will be surprised how feeling entitled to take your time will bolster your self-esteem and dignity and give you space to be honest with yourself.

It is worth adding here that even if we can think of a response in the moment, we still need to be careful. Our depth of processing makes us very aware of others and their flaws, so our incisive remarks, whilst based on a deep knowing, might hurt someone deeply. Therefore, it's always worth asking yourself if (a) a response is needed at all, (b) does this person realise how knowing and strong you are when they pick a fight with you? And (c) is it necessary to hurt someone to get your point across? Just because they feel it's OK to hurt someone, does that mean it is OK for you to do the same? As HSPs, being very familiar with our sensitivity and vulnerability, *we can sometimes forget how strong we are* and that our understanding of other people and our incisive questions can feel painfully sharp or pointed to others.

Another way to look after ourselves might be to create a kind of imaginary protective barrier around us. Some people like to imagine they are surrounded by white light that bounces the hurt or toxicity off them. Others use breathing and meditation to create a lasting and resilient sense of safety and openness. Thus when we are spending time with difficult people or situations, we could feel better resourced and protected. *The better we feel about ourselves, the less likely we are to take offence or to be bullied*, realising that other people's opinions say more about them than us. It can be a very good habit to approach the world on a daily basis with an intention to do no harm, to exude warmth and generosity and to welcome difference with curiosity.

23

CREATING OR CHOOSING HEALTHY WORK ENVIRONMENTS AND COMPATIBLE COLLEAGUES

For highly sensitive people, environment is everything, so it is not surprising if this might apply to our work and career choices. Our environment consists not only of a physical space, but the way it is set out. The kinds of sounds, light and smells we encounter will have an impact, as will comfort of furnishings, quality of equipment and the sense of purpose that is felt in the space. The kinds of boundaries, both in terms of behaviour, working hours and physical boundaries, will make a difference as well. In addition to that, a very important element of our work environment is the number and kind of people (and their emotions) that we interact with, how long we spend with them and the ethos or values that are operating within our physical and psychic space.

Even if we work from home, we are affected by our work

environment on many levels. Many HSPs find working environments stressful but often don't take into account that these environments exist through choice. It's important that HSPs interview companies that hire them and, if possible, the team that they will join, so that they will know if they fit in and if the work set-up will be good for them. For HSPs, meaning has at least as much value as financial reward, so check out the values and attitudes of any company or organisation before choosing them to influence many hours of your working week. Being intuitive, often HSPs are in a good position to work out if a workplace is healthy but they can only do this if they have an opportunity to have a good look and actually meet people who will be their bosses, co-workers and policy-makers. Don't be afraid to ask difficult questions: what is current staff turnover? Why did the last person leave? Are people encouraged to take breaks and vacation time? Is there the option of flexible working? What values are important to them? If they want someone who will be willing to work sixty hours a week or more and who will treat the 'bottom line' as the only criteria, maybe that workplace is not for you.

For many reasons, working for oneself, or working from home/hybrid working, is a popular choice for HSPs since they can influence their environment and pace their work to be able to give their best. You can choose your role as a self-employed worker, following your interests and developing your career path as you go along. If you work for yourself, you can put yourself on training and support events at will. Travel time is often reduced and scheduling is per the HSP's routine. HSPs tend to be quality-versus-quantity people, so if you are working for someone else, make sure that is acceptable to your employers or clients before you start. If you are self-employed, remember you can choose the companies or people you work with. For extrovert HSPs, this option of remote working might need careful planning so that you make sure you have opportunities to meet others and interact at times; you might not feel the benefit of this type of independence if you are feeling lonely or isolated or without the spark of face-to-face interactions in your work.

Be careful when weighing up family commitments. Having a young child in the home whilst you are working, even if you have someone else to look after them, can be astoundingly distracting for HSPs, who find it particularly difficult to ignore cues of need, distress, noises and interruptions. Furthermore, even though there is a lot more equality nowadays around women at work, they often still bear the burden of most of the domestic routine and emotional work within the household, so be mindful of this. Remember, the deep processing that is central to HSP functioning needs quiet space and that processing is also tiring, we are not robots.

The key to self-employment for HSPs is careful planning ahead of time, a diary that has breaks, vacation and rest time scheduled well in advance (which is sacrosanct), plus time for connection and interaction. In general, HSPs tend to need less than full-time hours to feel well. Remember this when you take on a new role and look for companies that are open to changing your hours to match needs outside of work as well as within the work environment. Companies that are too controlling, or do not have the imagination to perceive their employees as people with varied needs, will not be a good place for an HSP. You will need good self-discipline in order not to distract yourself also.

Bullying can come in many forms; even bosses can be bullied by underlings, so be aware of your boundaries and reasonable expectations of treatment by colleagues. For the most part, if an HSP is being bullied, it is better to leave sooner rather than later. If this is happening to you, use HR or union procedures if you need to, but don't hang in there too long; HSPs are more affected by negative environments. If people get up and leave toxic environments and join companies that are positive and healthy, eventually toxicity will bring about the demise of organisations that allow unhealthy dynamics to deplete their talented workforce. This is evolution and you can be at the forefront of it.

Before you leave, you can check that you have tried everything you can to resolve difficult dynamics. There is a good workbook called *How to Talk to Your Enemies at Work* by Alicia Dunams that offers help to navigate difficulties and improve communication and well-being within stressful work environments. It is natural for an HSP to feel a sense of loyalty and to want to see if they can change an environment from within, but remember that 80% of the workforce will not be as affected as you by toxicity, so even if you stand up for something, there might not be much support for you amongst colleagues who are not finding something as disturbing as you (yet).

Choose your career, or career change, wisely. Take time to think about what interests and motivates you, take time to study and learn new things, change your mind about what you want to do. Be prepared to make changes and take well-thought-out risks, rather than stay in a bad or boring environment and burn out. Beware of the influence of domestic partners and their expectations or needs, particularly their material ones, or overcommitting yourself financially at home, as this can limit your flexibility and options to leave a toxic workplace. Having savings or some kind of financial safety net can increase your sense of safety and power to make changes to protect your health.

24

MAKING CHOICES THAT MATCH WITH VALUES

The moral compass of HSPs is very strong and governs every choice they make. This is not an overstatement. However, there is often a lot of pressure on HSPs to 'be in the real world' and to compromise their natural wisdom for the short-term goals of the majority. An example of this is when HSPs, who tend to lean towards simple living, allow themselves to be persuaded to live a more materialistic lifestyle than is ideal for them and end up feeling stuck in an unfulfilling rat race.

People often assume that HSPs who hold certain values dear are out of touch with reality and perhaps naïve. Nothing could be further from the truth. In terms of values and integrity, HSPs are very mature. Their depth of processing enables them to bring an important perspective to both their own and others' lives. For this reason, they often make sound leaders and can keep integrity, which draws confidence from those they come into contact with.

From my own informal observations over thirty years,

the top three values that HSPs display in practice are: truth, kindness, fairness. Without exception, if an HSP is unhappy, it will be because something has happened that crosses those important values, either for them, or they have seen it happen for others and are strongly compelled to do something. This can apply in the home, in relationships and even at work. A lot of HSP social justice activists are moved towards this kind of work as a response to their innate sense of right and wrong, their compassion, integrity and perspective. What they often don't realise is that the organisations for which they work can sometimes miss how important it is to have the same attitudes to their own workforce. Your values should govern not only how you want others to be treated, but it should also govern the way in which you expect to be managed and treated yourself in any setting, whether at home or at work.

It is so important to consciously be aware of your own values when making choices, whether that is in your education, your choice of work, who you live with, how you manage your finances, where you shop and what behaviour you exhibit or tolerate. Try not to be pressured into things that 'everybody' does, just to fit in. At the same time, be aware that whilst you might notice injustice, it is not necessarily your job to do all the work of changing things twenty-four hours a day; maybe your role is simply to notice and speak about it. Many HSP social justice activists burn out within two years, this is because they often try to function in that world like the other 80%.

Be cautious with your energy and use it in ways that work for you. Perhaps in writing, organising, supporting, rather than putting yourself in the firing line. HSPs are more easily traumatised, so use discretion in your response to the crossing of your deeply held values. Also, take care to develop aspects of yourself such as non-judgment, communication skills and self-care, so that you can continue to act on your values with true integrity and compassion for others as well as yourself. *Remember that we are not supposed to 'fit in'. We are different for a reason.* The other 80% also have their role, so it's not our job to tell them what to do. However, we can provide opportunities and prompts for them to think about a different perspective or a different outcome. It is important not to underestimate our ability to influence, even when we are not in control.

Choose when and how you use your energy and pay attention to the environment.

25

DEALING WITH SELF-DOUBT

When I think about self-doubt, I often like to call this 'self-query'. Self-query is a sign of intelligence: one questions one's assumptions and looks at evidence. This is a very important ability, since it leads to good decisions and compassionate behaviour. It is not uncommon, however, for HSPs to be plagued with self-doubt. This is what happens when you find yourself at odds with a dominant culture, or if you are a minority. Additionally, I have often come across HSPs who deride their innate intuitive ability after absorbing the idea that intuition is connected to woolly thinking rather than logic or deductive thinking. Over time, they have lost trust in a part of themselves and this can interfere with their ability to feel confident in their own decision-making processes.

HSPs might sometimes wonder if the doubts or intuitive dialogue they can hear going on inside them can be trusted or relied upon. Since we are open to learning, it makes sense that we might listen carefully to another point of view or watch what is happening for other people and wonder if we might be wrong in our initial thoughts. This is a good starting place. However, it is important to then continue the enquiry to look at ourselves and work out whether our own ideas have ever been good ones, and if our decisions have been sound *for us*. Since we are the minority, it will make sense that when most people talk about what is best, they are talking about what is best for the majority or what is best *for them*. Others will not naturally have insight into what is good for us, what decisions will be best, since they do not have the same experiences as highly sensitive people. As HSPs, we often have a different route to goals, so we have to be discerning in who we listen to and the basis from which they make sense of the world.

When making decisions, or feeling doubtful about your interpretation of the world, the people in it, the pathways to our goals, always remember to examine the ideas from the standpoint of 'what is right for me in this moment?'. We may not fully understand why things feel different for us initially, and we can talk with other HSP friends or understanding therapists or coaches to check out our ideas. Remember, we often do know what the best thing to do is, but we tend to have a longer and more circuitous route to the resolution of our needs, hopes and quality of life. So give yourself not only some time but also accept that your decisions might depart from the path of the majority from time to time.

Whenever you are feeling doubtful, think back to the past when your intuition was telling you what was needed. Remember the times you ignored this and how things turned out, and remember the times you followed your intuition and how that turned out. Take particular note if you feel that your need to please others is causing you to ignore your intuition or causing you to make choices based solely on the needs or opinions of others; this kind of people-pleasing and dependence on others for direction can sometimes lead to a lack of experience in trusting our own process and our own mind.

Also remember that we don't have to rely solely on intuition. We can use our research abilities, reading, conversation with those wiser than ourselves to help make a decision that will work for us. Sometimes, there are many different choices and none of them is a bad one, and none of them are the 'best'. Many people will tell you that hindsight is a powerful thing, but until you have the magical ability to time travel, you will not be able to make the right decision every time. Just remember that science shows us that, overall, HSPs tend to make better decisions than the other 80%, so you are off to a good start already.

26

EAT AND SLEEP WELL

It is hard to imagine, but many HSPs actually allow their eating and sleeping needs to be dominated by what other people think it should be. HSPs need a couple of hours' extra sleep or rest than the other 80%; it's normal for them to go to bed earlier, to nap and to need uninterrupted sleep. It is particularly hard for HSPs, once they have started a family, to get good-quality sleep. Remember that your trait is high in deep processing, and your brain needs time to process your day, both consciously and during sleep. It can sometimes be useful to partner up with a cooperative and understanding non-HSP partner when having children, simply because they will not suffer quite so much as you when babies require feeding and changing in the night and can help out without experiencing such a depleting effect as you. In HSP–HSP relationships, be careful to plan well, so you both get some rest. When planning a family, have discussions about responsibilities and support and be specific about plans for how you will get enough sleep. Try not to be swayed by relatives who are not HSPs to set up routines or working hours that put too much pressure on your sleep needs or fail to give you enough quiet and downtime.

Food for HSPs makes a huge difference and it is not uncommon for HSPs to need supplements. When people are stressed, their gut can change and fail to digest nutrients satisfactorily, and a lot of HSPs are stressed because they are not yet living their authentic sensitive life. Nutrition is something that is hugely influential for everyone, but especially for HSPs, since we need plenty of nutrients for our very busy nervous system. HSPs require warm food to help that system calm itself and plenty of protein to help manage cortisol levels. Eat a good variety of foods, eat early in the evening rather than late at night, and be aware that due to HSPs' sensitivity to their own sugar levels, you might need to eat five small meals, rather than three larger ones. Eat something small and healthy at least every hour, even if that is a few nuts, or half a small banana, to keep your sugar levels stable. Take care with drinks such as coffee, black tea or alcohol, all of which have significant amounts of chemicals that affect your nervous system and, subsequently, your sleep. There are books, like Dr Ted Zeff's *The Highly Sensitive Person's Survival Guide: Essential Skills for Living Well in an Overstimulating World*, that can give you lots of guidance on health, food, sleep and much more. HSPs are known to respond more strongly or differently to some medications, so do bear this in mind when discussing medicine, dosage and treatments with your doctor. HSPs need medications, just like anyone else, but what we know about the HSP nervous system shows us that we need to be wise and gentle with ourselves, even with our medication. It stands to reason that we will also need to be thoughtful about any use of recreational drugs, especially any that do not come with a written list of ingredients.

27

HAVE FUN AND LAUGH, INCREASE JOY

For many HSPs, life can feel fairly serious. Not only are they aware of and affected by all the difficult things that are going on in the larger world around them, but they can also be affected by pressures to fit in and to meet expectations of the majority culture. HSPs' minds are often focused on problem-solving, which makes them very useful to the community, but if that problem-solving is active in all areas of life, this can create a negative experience. Given the right circumstances, HSPs can find humour and hilarity in many things, including in themselves, and I have often noticed HSPs' particular brand of 'silly' humour. I have heard it said that humour provides a very intelligent commentary on life, so let's not forget that we can be part of that commentary.

The expression of joy, laughter and fun are just as much the territory of HSPs as anyone else, but sometimes we can end up playing the role of the serious, responsible one, or perhaps finding ourselves on high alert trying to prevent things turning bad, being the monitor in relational terms. If that is the case, then we might miss out on the positive side of sensitivity, especially the experience of gathering together as sensitive people to have fun. It is wonderful to experience being in a group of HSPs fooling around, making jokes, giggling and otherwise being light-hearted. I believe this is as much the preserve of the HSP as the other 80%, if only we can relax and let go. It cannot be underestimated how important it is for us to find our humour and to have fun, since this is central to a healthy and happy nervous system and good physical and mental health in general.

Having fun on the beach with furry friends for company.

28

HAVE A BIGGER PICTURE PURPOSE, OR DISCOVER A BIGGER PICTURE PURPOSE FOR YOUR LIFE

HSPs will often step forward to fill a role that is needed; this can happen very quickly since we are highly attuned to what goes on around us and, consequently, the needs of others. Sometimes those roles we play can be a collection of very practical and small things in which we try to complete various helpful but small tasks for everyone around us; offering to do the school car pool, picking up groceries for someone, visiting lonely relatives, making sure our children have what they need in their backpacks. However, even though all these things are important, we can sometimes underestimate the usefulness of our perspective, our intelligence, wisdom, compassion and 'big-picture thinking' in performing other roles: maybe writing, job roles that require a lot of planning and understanding of complex issues, teaching, supporting, providing creative or original solutions within an organisation. We often forget that we might have a purpose beyond being kind or reliable; we also have emotional leadership to offer. Our wisdom is often something we seem to think should stay in our own head, not acknowledging that the purpose of this wisdom is to share it where it is needed. When you look at your life, and the minutiae, do you have a sense of a bigger purpose surrounding that and, if so, do you intentionally seek to align your activities and roles within that purpose? It is important to take time out to think about yourself and your role, where you stand in a bigger purpose, so that you can lead an authentic and congruent life and walk a spiritual as well as a practical path during your life. One doesn't have to be religious to be spiritual; it is a state of mind that connects us to something higher than our own needs, with a longer-term meaning that affects others.

> When you feel peaceful joy, that's when you are
> near truth.
>
> — RUMI

29

HAVE A PLAN FOR YOUR LIFE

Surprising numbers of HSPs, when looking back, realise that they have lived a life responding to other people, their expectations and what they think or need, rather than setting a map ahead for themselves leading to where they intuit they need to go. We are so tuned in to others that we pick up on both stark and subtle clues about expectations and values held by others. Once we embark on a path in life, we can then sometimes become stuck, overly burdened financially or overly responsible for other people's trajectories. When this happens, the world misses out on yet another fully fledged HSP, doing what they are designed to do: joining the majority and blending in instead of bringing their own refreshing and valuable input to a developing world.

We can encourage our highly sensitive children (HSC) to remember that their path might look different to the majority and they may, in fact, have interests that are quite different in terms of relationships, careers and ways of living. As parents, we need to encourage their difference whilst also supporting our HSCs to find ways to live within the world whilst not always being part of it. This can be complex, especially during teenage years, but it is worth taking the trouble to be truly supportive and understanding of the time it takes, and the complexity of decision-making for young sensitive people.

Even if we have found out about being an HSP in mid-life, we can still create a plan. It is never too late, but often we have more ingrained habits to break in order to follow our path as sensitive beings. We will probably have always known what we really should have been doing all our lives but perhaps lacked the support and understanding that was needed for us to follow our path. We are never too old to break free and to develop our sensitive gifts and perspective; remember that wisdom only increases with age. So it is worth sitting with a friend, a therapist or coach to look at how you want your continuing life map to look.

Take your time, don't let anyone rush you. Make sure your plan also contains flexibility to accommodate your growing maturity and needs. Accept that you might grieve decisions from the past but welcome the healing that will take place as a result of the expressions of your grief. Being real is the key to seeing the way forward and, having survived living in a world culture that was not designed with us in mind, we do have great strength and resilience. Where is your map leading?

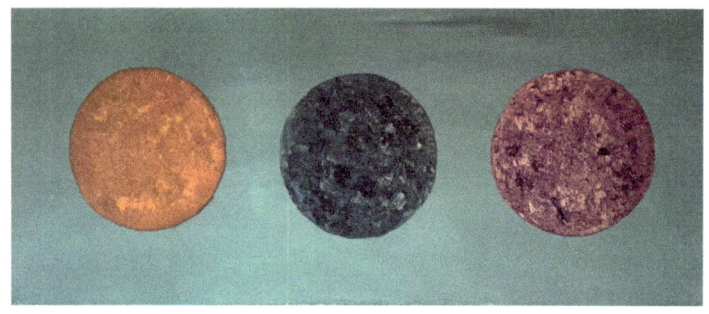

Follow your intuition and things will start to align.

30

USE EXERCISE
CONSTRUCTIVELY

$\mathcal{E}$veryone knows that exercise is good for us, but there is a wide variety of ways to do this. For some of us, we are sporty, we are physically strong or agile, and we get a lot of encouragement from the majority culture because we can garner feel-good experiences for them and us by competing, by demonstrating prowess and technique. Yet, not all of us are made to be physically able, so some of us might engage in walks in nature, gentler sports, yoga, non-competitive sports or undemanding forms of dance. The thing we need to be careful about is using exercise to manage our feelings in an unhelpful way. Exercise if often prescribed for low mood as a way to use the body's own chemicals to lift positive signals to the brain. But if we experience long-term anxiety or issues about self-identity, there is a possibility of using exercise as a form of control that has the potential to harm our bodies and create physical problems or addictions that serve only to disconnect us from what matters. We might even use exercise to manage stress instead of making fundamental changes that might change our life for the better.

Always make sure that you have a good balance in your exercise regime and see that it matches your body type and the type of things that make your heart sing. Being seen coming back from a ten-mile jog just so your sporty neighbour will think better of you is no substitute for feeling good about yourself for your own qualities. Notice whose feedback you are paying attention to and use your highly sensitive wisdom to check that all of this plays into your own set of values. Extreme competitiveness does not often suit highly sensitive people, since it encourages aggression and a win-lose mentality that can cause stress and damage our self-worth and that of others. Collaborative teamwork helps push forward achievements but be careful which sports you get yourself or your children involved in; make sure it is something that is loved and not just another stressful thing to add to an already stressful life. Take joy in movement, even if that is putting on some favourite music and dancing alone in your room; exercise is exercise, and no one should be telling you how much to do or how to do it unless you really need to know for your own reasons.

Remember that a lot of HSPs enjoy non-team sports, like jogging, walking, yoga or gardening and there is a reason for that: some pastimes offer a chance for reflection time that is not possible in team activities.

31

HONOUR AND GIVE SPACE FOR YOUR NATURAL RESPONSES TO WORLD EVENTS

As sensitive people, we are very well aware of the sad and worrying things that take place out there in the world. We have access to newspapers and news programs just like everyone else. However, we do process all of this information more deeply and our extra-busy mirror neurons play a part in the depth of our empathic response and understanding. It is perfectly fine if we sometimes need to go somewhere quiet and cry about what we see that is sad. This is natural for us and if we try to ignore it, we will become unwell. Although it is usual for the majority to listen to the news every day, many HSPs choose to listen once a week or even less, simply so that they have time to absorb the news and to filter and deeply process their feelings and thoughts around these things. Shocking news does not roll off our back like water on ducks; we need time to feel and think. We also need time to do what we do very well indeed; we seem to have an ability to make connections and find patterns in things and to see how what happens in the moment connects to past and future. This is part of the wisdom that HSPs hold for the rest of the community, but if we don't give ourselves time for this activity, we will not be able to be a voice of wisdom or ingenuity when it is needed. So don't feel bad if you find the news somewhat challenging or even grief-provoking at times. Take your time and recognise that being affected by this is a good thing and it happens for a reason. You are the voice of many when the powerful or greedy speak too loudly; you might speak gently, you might not speak often, but you can speak anyway, laying down seeds for the future.

32

EVALUATE, TEND AND HONOUR YOUR RELATIONSHIPS AT HOME AND AT WORK

*E*valuating relationships is essential as a form of personal housekeeping. Relationships can exist temporarily, or for a season, or for a lifetime, but each one is a choice for us to have, whether we understand that or not. HSPs are affected more than most people by their environments, and relationships are environments. So, if we keep negative people around us, we need to be aware that we will be affected more (differential susceptibility), whereas if we are surrounded by positive people, we will enjoy more benefit from that than most as well (this is called vantage sensitivity).

Staying in a toxic relationship with anyone is a habit that often forms in childhood and is something that can severely affect our progress in life and our day-to-day happiness. Quite a number of the HSPs I met during my twenty years as a therapist, who were seeing me for depression or anxiety or self-worth issues, were in relationships with people who were demanding, toxic, careless, developmentally challenged or unwilling to do the work of personal development (and holding them back as a result). Often the relationships had continued because the HSP mistook feeling compassion for them, for love. This is *not* love and it is certainly not self-love. We can stay in workplace relationships that are not serving us as well through a false sense of loyalty, fear of moving on, fear of change, fear of failure and imposter syndrome. Of course, there will always be some people in our lives that we currently feel we have to tolerate, but we need to remember that no one has a right to a permanent place in our lives if they are not living up to some basic standards of respect, care and general progress in life. If you are constantly tired and wired, finding it hard to sleep or often feeling tearful, think about how the various relationships and responsibilities in your life are affecting those feelings.

If you feel you might need to make some changes, you could try therapy or coaching or talking with a friend about how you could make a start in changing your life. Don't feel rushed, but don't procrastinate either. Start to behave like your real self *now*; that might help those people to move aside under their own steam as they find you less accommodating or you stop pretending something is not affecting you. You might, at the same time, find it helpful to start writing a list of the good things you bring to any type of relationship and what you expect so that you are balanced and aware of what you have to offer as a person and what you need.

When it comes to honouring and valuing the good relationships in your life, take a quick personal survey. How many good people do you count as friends in your life? What is it about them that you find attractive or nice to be around? Do you tend to find it easier to let down those who are nice more often than those in your life who are not, thus depriving yourself of the company of good people whilst spending too much time with those who make you feel unhappy or bored?

Do you tell those you value what it is about them that you adore or appreciate? Are you authentic and honest with your friends, even if this might cause a temporary conflict? Do you value yourself enough to invite someone good to spend time with you? Do you set aside time to grow those relationships? Are there people near to your inner circle whom you don't attempt to know better because you can't imagine them liking you, or maybe even because you feel a little envious of their lives, which seem full of positive energy and different to yours right now? It is worth sitting down quietly somewhere and thinking on all of this so that you don't miss out on the good things in people around you and the resources and friendship they can bring to your life. Whether you only see them when you buy a magazine, or whether they are someone that you have not previously recognised as providing something important in your life, they are there for you if you give yourself time to notice.

Carefully chosen friends will value you for your real self.

– BARBARA ALLEN – WILLIAMS

33

PURSUE BEAUTY AND HARMONY WHERE THEY OUGHT TO BE

HSPs seem to have the most poignant ability to see beauty where it is and to appreciate it. It is often the sensitive ones who show others what they miss in the rush and tear of life. This might be to point out the first daffodil of spring, or to stop and listen to the wind in the trees, or to take some time to reminisce on the childhood evocations of the smell of candyfloss or mown grass. Whatever you appreciate, whether it is art, poetry, music, the beauty of a baby's smile, the fragility and tensile strength of a spider's web, make the most of it and don't keep that appreciation to yourself. We are designed by nature to share how we are affected, so let it happen in a positive way whenever it feels right to do so.

Harmony to HSPs is like velvet: strongly woven yet soft to the touch. We respond instinctively to reclaim harmony amongst people, in colours, in design, in ideas, in nature, in so many things. It is in our nature to promote harmony, even in the most complex things, and it is such a common attribute of high sensitivity that I feel it has a purpose all of its own. Harmony counteracts destructive dynamics, so why would we not pursue harmony where we can? It is the perception of the discomfort of disharmony that often prods us into instinctive acts that bring people together, smooth over difficulties and create ever more beautiful art. Never underestimate your role in promoting harmony on any level, it can make the difference between life and death, not only of people but also of planets.

Harmony in nature is an inspiration not to be missed.

34

PREPARE TO PLANT SEEDS THAT WILL FLOURISH LONG AFTER YOU HAVE PLANTED THEM

Many HSPs say that they feel they have to stay quiet. Often, they feel that their emotional responses are looked down upon, or don't count as much as intellectual or logical responses. This is just not true. Your attention to the emotions that well up in you are vital if you are to understand the meaning of what you witness and the messages that are yours to share. Quite a few of us get hung up when we say something that others then proceed either to ignore or misunderstand, perhaps not even stopping to listen at all. However, this is not the point of having a deeply reflective nature or of planting seeds. Our seeds of wisdom need to be scattered far and wide. It is not our business whether they take root or sprout. Some seeds can take one hundred years to germinate, but we still need to plant seeds. Our minds are well designed to create new things, to develop understanding and wisdom, so we need to use our voices to share our deep processing and our observations, even if, at the time, no one seems to value what we say. The cost to the world if we fail to say what is in our hearts and minds, is a continued pursuit of negative or short-term planning that affects all of us, now and for centuries in the future.

A forest can start with a single seed...

35

RESOURCES

Barbara's resources

Workshop and discussion cards

During the process of writing this book, I have also created a pack of flash cards called 'One in Five Hidden Treasures'©, which can be used by HSPs for group discussion prompts or can be adapted as cards for each day, to offer you something to think about as you live your daily life. You can find out about those cards on my website at www.growingunlimited.co.uk.

HSP events

Since 2009, I have been facilitating group experiences for HSPs, so you might occasionally see a workshop on my Meetup site (Growing Unlimited HSP Meetup). Do come along to one of those if you would like to; not just for the work but to meet others like yourself who might turn out to be the new friends you thought you would never have.

Facebook

You can find me on Facebook (Barbara Allen-Williams) and I also have a Facebook page called 'Growing Unlimited Centre for High Sensitivity'.

Other resources:

One of the long-standing recurring events that I recommend is the 'HSP Gathering Retreat', co-founded by Jacquelyn Strickland and Elaine Aron in 2001. These five-day events are held in the USA and around the world. They are perfect opportunities to commune with other HSPs whilst addressing topics that are the heart and soul of HSP life. You can find out more about these unique gatherings at www.jacquelynstrickland.com.

Books

Books that might be useful for HSPs, about high sensitivity and personal development in general:

The Highly Sensitive Person: How to Survive and Thrive When The World Overwhelms You by Elaine Aron. This is the seminal book about HSPs, which is a must-read for any highly sensitive person.

The Highly Sensitive Child: A Comprehensive Parenting Guide for Raising Confident and Capable Children by Elaine Aron. This is a must-read for anyone raising or working with highly sensitive children.

The Highly Sensitive Person in Love: Understanding and Managing Relationships when the World Overwhelms You by Elaine Aron. Succinctly describes the highly sensitive person in intimate relationships, with many suggestions for interacting with HSPs and non-HSPs.

The Highly Sensitive Person's Workbook by Elaine Aron. Offers specific exercises for reframing your life as an HSP; many suggestions for coping and information on how to start your own HSP discussion group.

The Highly Sensitive Parent: How to Care for Your Kids When You Care Too Much by Elaine N Aron, PhD. A self-help book for the significant number of parents who are unusually attuned to their children.

The Undervalued Self: Restore Your Love/Power Balance, Transform the Inner Voice That Holds You Back and Find Your True Self-Worth by Elaine N Aron, PhD.

Psychotherapy and the Highly Sensitive Person: Improving Outcomes for That Minority of People Who Are the Majority of Clients by Elaine N Aron, PhD.

The Strong, Sensitive Boy: Help Your Son Become a Happy, Confident Man by Ted Zeff.

The Highly Sensitive Person's Survival Guide: Essential Skills for Living Well in an Overstimulating World by Ted Zeff, PhD.

Highly Sensitive Person's Companion: Daily Exercises for Calming Your Senses in an Overstimulating World by Ted Zeff, PhD.

The Artists Way: A Course in Discovering and Recovering Your Creative Self by Julia Cameron.

The Art of Extreme Self-Care: Transform Your Life One Month at a Time by Cheryl Richardson. Insightful and inspiring.

An Adult Child's Guide to What's Normal by John and

Linda Friel. If you were brought up in a dysfunctional family, how do you know what expectations, feelings and behaviours are normal, in yourself and others? Help from the ground up, with healing and recovery.

The Career Guide for Creative and Unconventional People by Carol Eikelberry. A helpful guide with inspiring insights for anyone who feels they don't fit or want the usual career pattern.

The Highly Sensitive Man by Tom Falkenstein. An up-to-date, informed and helpful book on SPS and the men who make up half of the HSP population. Written by a cognitive behavioural therapist.

Confessions of a Highly Sensitive Man by William Allen. A unique and compassionate perspective on his journey, struggles and evolution as a highly sensitive man.

Making Work Work for the Highly Sensitive Person by Barrie Jaeger. A comprehensive look at identifying your skills and gifts as a sensitive person and how to make work life better for you.

Your Rainforest Mind: A Guide to the Well-Being of Gifted Adults and Youth by Paula Prober.

Social Justice for the Sensitive Soul: How to Change the World in Quiet Ways by Dorcas Cheng-Tozun. Thinks about how sensitive people can make a difference without the crash and burn.

The Road Less Traveled by Scott M Peck. Wisdom about what is required if we want to grow and how that happens.

Thrill! by Tracy M Cooper, PhD. About the high sensation seeking, highly sensitive person, maximising potential and balancing the challenges.

Thrive! by Tracy M Cooper, PhD. The highly sensitive person and career. For HSPs who wish to move beyond surviving at work.

The Anxiety Sisters: How You Can Become More Hopeful, Connected and Happy by Abbe Greenberg and Maggie Sarachek. Informative, practical and humorous.

Sensitive: The Power of Feeling in a World that Doesn't by Hannah Jane Walker. Overturns old clichés and stereotypes to give a new perspective of sensitivity as an essential strength.

The Bridge: A Nine-Step Plan to Healing Your Trauma, Accepting Yourself and Living Life to the Full by Donna Lancaster. A book about grief.

The Power of Vulnerability: Teachings of Authenticity, Connection, and Courage by Brene Brown. Brown emphasises that embracing vulnerability can help us lead fulfilling lives with wholeheartedness.

How to Talk to Your Enemies: 101+ Ways to Turn Hostility into Peace by Alicia Dunams. Discover specific words, phrases, and approaches to start dialogues off on the right foot toward mutual understanding and healing. There is also a workbook that goes with this.

Articles, papers, movies and newsletters

Some of the very best articles and up-to-date research papers can be found on Elaine Aron, PhD's website at www.hsperson.com. There is a search box if you are looking for something on a particular HSP topic.

Elaine Aron releases newsletters from time to time, including information about current research and her encouraging perspective on the challenges and joys of the HSP trait. Jacquelyn Strickland also has a newsletter full of useful articles, information and support. You can sign up for these newsletters by going to their websites.

Here are some papers that might be good to start you off:

Aron, E. & Aron, A. (1997). Sensory-processing sensitivity and its relation to introversion and emotionality, *Journal of Personality and Social Psychology, 73, 345–368.*

Prochaska & DiClemente, (1983). Stages of Change Model

Silverman, L. (1994). 'The Moral Sensitivity of Gifted Children and the Evolution of Society'.

Wilson, D S., Coleman, K., Clark, A B., & Beideman, L (1993). Shy-bold continuum in pumpkinseed sunfish (*Lepomis gibbonsus*): An ecological study of a psychological trait. *Journal of Comparative Psychology, 107, 250–260.*

Barbara Allen-Williams. *Thoughts on High Sensitivity.* A number of short pieces of writing on aspects of high sensitivity and how we live. www.growingunlimited. co.uk

Charlotte Sheridan (2021). The tyranny of the 'shoulds', (a phrase coined by Karen Horney). There is a good article on www.theroompsy.com that explores this.

A movie about high sensitivity based on Elaine Aron's explanations of high sensitivity – *Sensitive, The Untold Story* – well worth watching.

Websites

Elaine N Aron, PhD: www.hsperson.com

Prof Michael Pluess and his team (UK):
    www.sensitivityresearch.co.uk

Barbara Allen-Williams: www.growingunlimited.co.uk

Jacquelyn Strickland: www.jacquelynstrickland.com

Personality self-assessments: www.16personalities.com

William Allen – Highly Sensitive Men:
    www.thesensitiveman.com

ABOUT THE AUTHOR

*B*arbara began working as a therapist in 1993. She retired from private practice in 2013 after twenty years as a therapist, supervisor and group worker. She focused on addictions until 2003, then moved to high sensitivity for the next ten years. Since 2013, she has been a mentor for highly sensitive people and a trainer and speaker in the specialist area of sensory processing sensitivity (a trait characterised by a stronger response to environmental stimuli). She is the founder and currently works at Growing Unlimited Consultancy (since 2002). Barbara was a founding director at the National Centre for High Sensitivity CIC in the UK (2010–2019). Her aim is to increase awareness for highly sensitive people generally and to help therapists, teachers, nursery staff, social workers and employers to be able to identify adults or children with SPS (sensory processing sensitivity), to be aware of their particular needs and, above all, their considerable strengths.

Barbara attended training directly with Dr Elaine Aron in San Francisco, USA, and is a founding member of ICHS (International Consultant on High Sensitivity). She has worked with individuals, groups and professionals nationwide, in Europe and the USA, educating and supporting. Barbara has participated numerous times as a co-host at HSP Gathering Retreats (founded by Elaine Aron, PhD and Jacquelyn Strickland in 2001). These retreats have taken place in the USA and Europe and are still continuing. There is a lot of work still to do in raising awareness around this trait and she is hoping that her events, courses and this book will assist in that process, making it easier for professionals to get the most from their work with sensitive individuals and for HSPs themselves to thrive and take positions of influence.

This book is based on Barbara's accumulated understanding and experience, during the last thirty years, of the challenges highly sensitive people face as they move towards maturity as human beings.

Barbara works from two different locations in the UK (Andover in Hampshire and Pendeen in Cornwall). Barbara was born in Cornwall and spent most of her young childhood able to roam free in nature around the beautiful far south-west coast of Cornwall. She loves writing, painting, gardening and cooking whenever she has the time. Now semi-retired, she spends time with her family and two dogs, interspersed with trips to the USA as a co-host at HSP Gathering Retreats. Barbara has four grown-up children and two grandchildren. Her husband Mike (the only non-HSP/HSS in the household!) has been a loving support and companion for more than twenty-five years.

More about Barbara and her work can be found at www.growingunlimited.co.uk and on Facebook, both under her own name and as Growing Unlimited.

View from Barbara's house in Pendeen.